# Solve Your Money Problems Now and Get Your Money Right!

### Allen P. Stevenson Ph.D.

Solve Your Money Problems Now and Get Your Money Right!

All rights reserved. No part of this book may be reproduced, stored in a retrieval system, or transmitted in any form or by any means, electronic, mechanical, photocopying, recording, or otherwise, without the prior written permission of the copyright owner.

Copyright © Allen P. Stevenson Ph.D. 2022

Solve Your Money Problems Now and Get Your Money Right!
## **TABLE OF CONTENTS**

INTRODUCTION

CHAPTER ONE: BUDGETING 101

CHAPTER TWO: SAVING FOR THE FUTURE

CHAPTER THREE: DEBT MANAGEMENT

CHAPTER FOUR: INVESTING FOR THE FUTURE

CHAPTER FIVE: REAL-LIFE EXAMPLES

CHAPTER SIX: COMMON MONEY MISTAKES AND HOW TO AVOID THEM

    Mistake 1: Not having a budget

    Mistake 2: Not saving enough for the future

    Mistake 3: Not paying off debt

    Mistake 4: Not investing wisely

    Mistake 5: Not shopping around for the best deal

    Mistake 6: Not having an emergency fund

CHAPTER SEVEN: CONCLUSION

# INTRODUCTION

In this book, we will explore the various financial challenges that many people face and provide practical solutions for overcoming them. We will delve into topics such as budgeting, saving, debt management, and investing, and provide real-life examples to illustrate the concepts and strategies discussed.

The purpose of this book is to help you take control of your financial life and make smart, informed decisions about your money. Whether you are struggling to pay off debt, save for a big purchase, or simply want to improve your financial literacy, this book is designed to provide you with the tools and knowledge you need to succeed.

So, if you are ready to get your money right, let us dive in!

*Solve Your Money Problems Now and Get Your Money Right!*

# CHAPTER ONE: BUDGETING 101

Budgeting is the foundation of good financial management. It involves creating a plan for how you will allocate your income and expenses over a period. By creating a budget, you can better understand where your money is going, identify areas where you may be overspending, and make adjustments to reach your financial goals.

Creating a budget starts with tracking your income and expenses. To do this, you will need to gather all of your financial statements, such as pay stubs, bank statements, and credit card statements. From there, you can categorize your expenses into different categories, such as housing, transportation, food, and entertainment. This will allow you to see where the majority of your money is going and identify any areas where you may be able to cut back.

Once you have a clear picture of your income and expenses, you can then create a budget that aligns with your financial goals. For example, if you are trying to pay off debt, you may need to allocate a larger portion of your budget toward debt repayment. If you are trying to save for a down payment on a house, you may need to cut back on non-essential expenses to free up more money for saving.

The key to successful budgeting is consistency. It is important to review and update your budget regularly, to ensure that you are staying on track and making progress toward your financial goals.

Here are a few steps for creating a budget:
- **Gather your financial statements:** Start by gathering all of your financial statements, including your income, expenses, debts, and savings.

- **Categorize your expenses:** Next, categorize your expenses into different categories, such as rent, groceries, entertainment, and debt repayment. This will help you see where your money is going and identify areas where you can cut back on expenses.

- **Create a plan:** Based on your income and expenses, create a plan for how you will allocate your money each month. Make sure to include your financial goals, such as saving for a down payment on a house or paying off debt.

- **Track your progress:** It is important to track your progress and make adjustments to your budget as needed. This can help you stay on track and reach your financial goals.

By following these steps and consistently reviewing and adjusting your budget, you can take control of your money and work towards a secure financial future. It is important to be patient and consistent in your approach and to continuously review and adjust your budget as your circumstances change.

# CHAPTER TWO: SAVING FOR THE FUTURE

Saving for the future is a crucial part of good financial management. It allows you to set aside money for emergencies, big purchases, and retirement.

There are many different reasons why people save, some of which include:

- **Building an emergency fund:** An emergency fund is a savings account that you set aside specifically for unexpected expenses, such as a medical bill or car repair. It is a good idea to have at least three to six months' worth of living expenses saved up in case of an emergency.

- **Saving for a down payment on a house:** If you are planning to buy a home in the future, it is important to start saving for a down payment as early as possible. A down payment is typically a percentage of the purchase price that you need to put down upfront. The larger the down payment, the smaller the mortgage loan you will need to take out, which can save you money on interest in the long run.

- **Saving for retirement:** Retirement may seem like a long way off, but it is never too early to start saving for it. There are many different options for investing for retirement, including 401(k) plans, IRAs, and individual brokerage accounts. It is important to consult with a financial advisor to determine the best strategy for your individual situation.

By setting aside money for the future, you can protect yourself against financial emergencies and work towards achieving long-term goals such as retirement.

Here are a few strategies for saving for the future:
- **Set financial goals:** Before you start saving, it is important to identify your financial goals and create a plan for how you will reach them. This will help you stay motivated and focused on your savings efforts.

- **Create a budget:** A budget can help you understand where your money is going and identify areas where you can cut back on expenses in order to free up more money for saving.

- **Automate your savings:** One of the easiest ways to save consistently is to set up automatic transfers from your checking account to your savings account. This way, you can save without having to think about it.

- **Invest for the long term:** In addition to saving in a traditional savings account, consider investing for the long term. By investing in a diversified portfolio of stocks, bonds, and mutual funds, you can potentially earn a higher return over the long term. However, it's important to understand that investing carries inherent risks and to consult with a financial advisor before making any investment decisions.

- **Learn to Use Coupons**: There is no shame in using product coupons. They do not symbolize an inability to afford a product. Rather, coupons are a widely accepted means to discount product purchases. You should try to get coupons from various sources, whether from the papers or the internet.

- **Avoid Financially Demanding Addictions**: Whether tobacco, alcohol, narcotic drugs, or gambling, addictions prevent effective saving. If you rather saved the funds used to fund your addiction, you will live a more financially comfortable life.

- **Consider a Meal Schedule:** A planned meal course is an unconventional saving strategy. Set a schedule for eating breakfasts, lunch, and dinner, as opposed to spontaneous or binge-feeding. This will have you save better. Also, home-prepared meals are considered more cost-effective than patronizing eateries. Hence the coat associated with such eateries can be channeled toward achieving your saving goals.

- **Developing Skills You Would Rather Pay For:** Developing money-demanding skills can help you save more and stay on top of your finances. Skills like Shampoo making, drawing, painting, internal decoration, and braiding, are all areas you can save money by doing yourself.

- **Occasional Thrift Shopping**: It is never a bad idea to thrift your way to financial independence. Products are not always inferior because they have been previously used. You can acquire valuable products at a subsidized rate in a thrift store, rather than spend heavily at expensive stores and online marketplaces. This creates more room to achieve your saving goals.

- **Effectively Manage Utility and Subscription Costs**: Rather than pay exorbitant utility bills, why not manage your energy usage? Passive behavior like switching off the lights or power-consuming devices when not used can go a long way to save cost. Also regulating internet usage can help you pay less on internet bills, and reserve more funds for savings. If you have a cable subscription, why not subscribe to a cheaper package if you do not watch all the channels on your existing package?

By consistently saving, and investing for the future, you achieve your financial goals and build a secure financial future. However, it is important to be patient and consistent in your journey. As they say, even Rome was not built in a day. You must make up your mind to be diligent. Continuously review your strategies and adjust your plan as your circumstances change.

# CHAPTER THREE: DEBT MANAGEMENT

Managing debt can be a tremendously difficult challenge for many people. Whether it is credit card debt, a student loan, or a mortgage, debt can be overwhelming and difficult to pay off. If you struggle with debt management, it is important to know that you can strategize your way out of indebtedness. With a good debt management plan, you can work towards paying off your debts and getting your finances back on track.

The first step towards effective debt management is understanding your debt. You must make a list of all of your debts, including the creditor, interest rate, and minimum monthly payment. This will give you a clear picture of what you owe and to whom.

Next, prioritize your debts. It is generally a good idea to focus on paying off high-interest debts first, as they will cost you more in the long run. You can also consider consolidating your debts to reduce numerous debt obligations, ease the repayment process, and possibly reduce interest costs. This can be achieved by taking out a single loan to pay off multiple debts.

It's also important to review your budget and see where you can cut back on expenses in order to free up more money for debt repayment. This may involve making sacrifices in the short term, but it will be worth it in the long run when you're able to pay off your debts and improve your financial situation.

If you have a significant amount of debt, it can be overwhelming and difficult to keep up with the monthly payments. However, ignoring debt can have serious consequences, including damaging your credit score and costing you more in interest over time.

Here are a few strategies for managing debt:
- **Create a budget:** Budgeting is key to understanding expenditures and identifying cost-cutting strategies. No one can manage their debt unless they have a superior understanding of their financial standing. What comes in? What goes out? What can be retained? and how can the money be channeled toward your debt obligations?

- **Prioritize your debts:** It is important to prioritize your debts and focus on paying off the ones with the highest interest rates first. Considering that debt with higher interest obligations costs much more in the long run, it will be important to pay off such debts first. This will help you save money on interest and pay off competing debts more quickly.

- **Consider Consolidation**: If you have multiple debts with high-interest rates, you can consider consolidating your debts to reduce numerous debt obligations, ease the repayment process, and possibly reduce interest costs. This can be achieved by taking out a single loan to pay off your debts and improve your financial situation.

- **Seek professional help:** If you are struggling to manage your debts, consider seeking help from a professional such as a financial advisor or credit counselor. They can help you create a customized debt management plan and provide guidance on how to get your debts under control.

It is important to be patient and consistent in your approach and to continuously review and adjust your plan as your circumstances change.

By following a consistent debt repayment plan and making smart financial decisions, you can work towards paying off your debts and improving your financial situation.

# CHAPTER FOUR: INVESTING FOR THE FUTURE

Investing is an incredible way to grow your wealth over time by putting your money into assets that have the potential to increase in value. There are several investment options, including stocks, bonds, mutual funds, and real estate. Investing can potentially increase your income sources, and position you to depend less on your paycheck. A financially minded person must know how to save enough to invest. More importantly, you must be able to consistently re-invest as investing is a lifetime project.

Before you start investing, it is important to have a clear understanding of your financial goals and risk tolerance. You should genuinely consider whether you are circumstantially disposed to make long-term or short-term investments. Also, whether you can afford to take high risks and generate more returns, or low risks and generate moderate returns over time. For example, young people with long-term investment goals may be more comfortable taking on high-risk investments in exchange for higher returns. If you are close to retirement, you may be more conservative in your investment choices in order to protect the money you have saved so far.

It is also important to diversify your investments. This means investing in a range of different asset classes in order to spread out your risk. For example, rather than putting all of your money into a single stock, you might invest in a diverse portfolio of stocks, bonds, and mutual funds.

Investing in your future is an important part of good financial management. By investing your money, you can potentially earn a higher return over the long term than you would by keeping your money in a savings account or other low-risk investment. However, investing carries inherent risks, and it is important to be informed and make smart investment decisions.

Here are a few statistics to consider when it comes to investing:

- **The stock market has historically provided a higher return over the long term than other types of investments:** According to the S&P 500 index, which tracks the stock performance of 500 large publicly traded companies, the annualized return over the past ninety (90) years has been around 9.8%.

- **Diversification is key to successful investing:** By investing in a variety of assets, such as stocks, bonds, and mutual funds, you can spread out your risk and potentially earn a higher return over the long term. The big advantage of diversifying is that there is an increased chance of one or more asset classes producing impressive returns.

- **Time is on your side when it comes to investing:** The longer you stay invested, the more time your money has to grow. For example, if you invest $10,000 in the stock market at an average annual return of 9.8% and leave it invested for 30 years, it could potentially grow to over $96,000.

By understanding the potential benefits and risks of investing, you can make informed decisions about your money and work towards reaching your long-term financial goals. It is important to consult with a financial advisor and create a diversified investment portfolio that aligns with your risk tolerance and financial goals.

It is important to be patient and disciplined in your investing approach. The stock market can be volatile in the short term, but over the long term, it has historically delivered solid returns. By staying invested for the long haul, you'll be more likely to achieve your financial goals.

# CHAPTER FIVE: REAL-LIFE EXAMPLES

Throughout this book, we have discussed various personal finance strategies. To bring these concepts to life, let us take a look at a few real-life examples of people who have successfully implemented these strategies in order to improve their financial situation.

**Example 1:**
Sara is a 28-year-old recent college graduate who is struggling with high levels of student loan debt. She has multiple loans with different interest rates, and she is finding it difficult to keep up with the monthly payments.

Sara decides to take action and create a debt management plan. She gathers all of her financial statements and creates a budget to see where her money is going. She then prioritizes her debts and focuses on paying off the loans with the highest interest rates first.

Sara also makes adjustments to her budget to free up more money for debt repayment. She cuts back on non-essential expenses, such as eating out and subscription services, and redirects that money toward her debts.

By following a consistent debt repayment plan and making smart financial decisions, Sara is able to pay off her student loans and get her finances back on track.

**Example 2:**
Jack is a 35-year-old software developer who is saving for a down payment on a house. He currently rents an apartment, but he is ready to take the next step and become a homeowner.

Jack creates a budget and identifies areas where he can cut back on expenses in order to free up more money for saving. He also sets up an automatic transfer from his checking account to his savings account every month, which helps him consistently save towards his goal.

In addition to saving for a down payment, Jack also starts investing for the long term. He consults with a financial advisor and creates a diversified portfolio of stocks, bonds, and mutual funds.

By consistently saving and investing, Jack is able to reach his goal of saving for a down payment on a house and also build wealth for the future.

**Example 3:**
Maria is a 45-year-old marketing manager who is looking to build wealth for retirement. She has a 401(k) through her employer, but she is looking for additional ways to invest for the long term.

Maria does some research and decides to open an individual brokerage account in addition to her 401(k). She consults with a financial advisor and creates a diversified portfolio of stocks and mutual funds.

Maria is disciplined in her investing approach and stays invested for the long term, even through market ups and downs. As a result, she's able to build a solid foundation for her retirement and achieve her financial goals.

**Example 4:**
Tom is a 27-year-old marketing assistant who has just started his first full-time job. He's excited about his new career, but he's also a little overwhelmed by the responsibility of managing his own finances for the first time.

Tom decides to take control of his money by creating a budget. He gathers all of his financial statements and categorizes his expenses into different categories, such as rent, groceries, and entertainment. He then creates a plan for how he will allocate his income each month in order to cover his expenses and meet his financial goals.

Tom's budget helps him understand where his money is going and identify areas where he can cut back on expenses. For example, he realizes that he's spending a lot of money on takeout and decides to start cooking more at home in order to save money. He also sets up automatic savings transfers to help him consistently save towards his financial goals.

By creating a budget and making smart financial decisions, Tom is able to take control of his money and get his finances on track.

**Example 5:**
Katie is a 32-year-old teacher who is saving for a down payment on a house. She currently rents an apartment, but she's ready to take the next step and become a homeowner.
Katie creates a budget and identifies areas where she can cut back on expenses in order to free up more money for

saving. She also sets up an automatic transfer from her checking account to her savings account every month, which helps her consistently save towards her goal.

In addition to saving for a down payment, Katie also starts investing for the long term. She consults with a financial advisor and creates a diversified portfolio of stocks, bonds, and mutual funds.

By consistently saving and investing, Katie is able to reach her goal of saving for a down payment on a house and also build wealth for the future.

**Example 6:**
Jessica is a 40-year-old small business owner who has accumulated a significant amount of credit card debt. She's finding it difficult to keep up with the monthly payments and is worried about the impact on her credit score.

Jessica decides to take action and create a debt management plan. She gathers all of her financial statements and creates a budget to see where her money is going. She then prioritizes her debts and focuses on paying off the credit cards with the highest interest rates first.

Jessica also makes adjustments to her budget to free up more money for debt repayment. She cuts back on non-essential expenses, such as dining out and subscription services, and redirects that money toward her debts.

By following a consistent debt repayment plan and making smart financial decisions, Jessica is able to pay off her credit card debt and get her finances back on track.

**Example 7:**
John is a 50-year-old engineer who is looking to build wealth for retirement. He has a 401(k) through his employer, but he's looking for additional ways to invest for the long term.

John does some research and decides to open an individual brokerage account in addition to his 401(k). He consults with a financial advisor and creates a diversified portfolio of stocks and mutual funds.

John is disciplined in his investing approach and stays invested for the long term, even through market ups and downs. As a result, he's able to build a solid foundation for his retirement and achieve his financial goals.

**Example 8:**

Esther is a 25-year-old recent college graduate who has just started her first full-time job. She's excited about her new career, but she's also a little overwhelmed by the responsibility of managing her own finances for the first time.

Esther decides to take control of her money by creating a budget. She gathers all of her financial statements and categorizes her expenses into different categories, such as rent, groceries, and entertainment. She then creates a plan for how she will allocate her income each month in order to cover her expenses and meet her financial goals.

Esther's budget helps her understand where her money is going and identify areas where she can cut back on expenses. For example, she realizes that she's spending a lot of money on takeout and decides to start cooking more at home in order to save money. She also sets up automatic savings transfers to help her consistently save towards her financial goals.

By creating a budget and making smart financial decisions, Esther is able to take control of her money and get her finances on track.

## Example 9:

Mike is a 35-year-old software developer who is saving for a down payment on a house. He currently rents an apartment, but he's ready to take the next step and become a homeowner.

Mike creates a budget and identifies areas where he can cut back on expenses in order to free up more money for saving. He also sets up an automatic transfer from his checking account to his savings account every month, which helps him consistently save towards his goal.

In addition to saving for a down payment, Mike also starts investing for the long term. He consults with a financial advisor and creates a diversified portfolio of stocks, bonds, and mutual funds.

By consistently saving and investing, Mike is able to reach his goal of saving for a down payment on a house and also build wealth for the future.

These are just a few examples of how individuals have successfully implemented the financial strategies discussed in this book. By budgeting, saving, managing debt, and investing wisely, you can take control of your financial situation and work towards a secure financial future.

**Example 10:**

Lisa is a 38-year-old graphic designer who has accumulated a significant amount of credit card debt. She's finding it difficult to keep up with the monthly payments and is worried about the impact on her credit score.

Lisa decides to take action and create a debt management plan. She gathers all of her financial statements and creates a budget to see where her money is going. She then prioritizes her debts and focuses on paying off the credit cards with the highest interest rates first.

Lisa also makes adjustments to her budget to free up more money for debt repayment. She cuts back on non-essential expenses, such as dining out and subscription services, and redirects that money toward her debts.

In addition to making changes to her budget, Lisa also looks into consolidation options. She decides to consolidate her credit card debt into a personal loan with a lower interest rate, which helps her save money on interest and makes it easier to pay off her debts.

By following a consistent debt repayment plan and making smart financial decisions, Lisa is able to pay off her credit card debt and get her finances back on track.

**Example 11:**
David is a 30-year-old marketing manager who is struggling to make ends meet. He's finding it difficult to pay his bills and is worried about falling behind on his debts.

David decides to take control of his money by creating a budget. He gathers all of his financial statements and categorizes his expenses into different categories, such as rent, groceries, and entertainment. He then creates a plan for how he will allocate his income each month in order to cover his expenses and meet his financial goals.

David's budget helps him understand where his money is going and identify areas where he can cut back on expenses. For example, he realizes that he's spending a lot of money on unnecessary subscription services and decides to cancel them in order to save money. He also sets up automatic savings transfers to help him consistently save towards his financial goals.

By creating a budget and making smart financial decisions, David is able to take control of his money and get his finances on track.

# CHAPTER SIX: COMMON MONEY MISTAKES AND HOW TO AVOID THEM

As you work towards improving your financial situation, it's important to be aware of common money mistakes that can set you back. Here are a few examples of common money mistakes and tips on how to avoid them:

**Mistake 1: Not having a budget**

A budget is a crucial tool for managing your money and reaching your financial goals. Without a budget, it's easy to overspend and end up in debt. To avoid this mistake, take the time to create a budget that outlines your income and expenses and helps you stay on track.

Without a budget, it's easy to lose track of where your money is going. Make sure to create a budget and track your expenses in order to stay on track and reach your financial goals.

## Mistake 2: Not saving enough for the future

Saving for the future is an essential part of good financial management. However, many people don't save enough, leaving themselves vulnerable to financial emergencies or unable to reach long-term goals such as retirement. To avoid this mistake, make saving a priority and consistently set aside money for the future.

It's important to save for the future in order to protect yourself against financial emergencies and work towards achieving long-term goals. Make sure to set aside a portion of your income for saving and invest for the long term in a diversified portfolio.

## Mistake 3: Not paying off debt

Debt can be overwhelming, and it's easy to fall behind on payments. However, ignoring debt can have serious consequences, including damaging your credit score and costing you more in interest over time. To avoid this mistake, create a debt management plan and work towards paying off your debts as quickly as possible.

High-interest debt, such as credit card debt, can be costly and take a long time to pay off. Make sure to focus on paying off high-interest debt first and consider consolidation options if necessary.

## Mistake 4: Not investing wisely

Investing can be a great way to grow your wealth over time, but it's important to be informed and make smart investment decisions. Avoiding this mistake involves doing your research, consulting with a financial advisor, and diversifying your portfolio to spread out risk.

## Mistake 5: Not shopping around for the best deal

It's important to shop around and compare prices before making a purchase. This can help you save money and get the best value for your money.

## Mistake 6: Not having an emergency fund

An emergency fund is a set of savings that you can use in case of unexpected expenses, such as a car repair or medical bill. Make sure to set aside a portion of your income for an emergency fund and aim to save enough to cover at least three to six months of living expenses.

By being aware of these common money mistakes and taking steps to avoid them, you can set yourself up for financial success. These common money mistakes that people make can have a negative impact on their financial well-being.

By avoiding these common money mistakes and making smart financial decisions, you can work towards a secure financial future. It's important to be patient and consistent in your approach and to continuously review and adjust your financial plan as your circumstances change.

# CHAPTER SEVEN: CONCLUSION

In this book, we have covered the basics of good financial management, including budgeting, saving, debt management, and investing. We have also looked at real-life examples of individuals who have successfully implemented these strategies in order to improve their financial situation. By implementing these strategies and making informed decisions about your money, you can take control of your financial life and work towards a secure financial future.

Remember, good financial management is a journey, not a destination. It's important to be patient and consistent in your approach and to continuously review and adjust your financial plan as your circumstances change.

We hope that the information and strategies presented in this book have been helpful in getting you started on your financial journey. With the right mindset and a solid plan in place, you can solve your money problems now and get your money right!

If you are looking for additional resources to help you improve your financial situation, here are a few suggestions:

- **Personal finance blogs and websites:** There are many personal finance blogs and websites that offer valuable advice and information on a range of financial topics. Some popular options include The Simple Dollar, NerdWallet, and Money Under 30.

- **Financial planning tools and apps:** There are a variety of financial planning tools and apps available that can help you track your budget, save money, and make informed financial decisions. Some popular options include Mint, YNAB (You Need a Budget), and Acorns.

- **Financial advisors:** If you're looking for more personalized guidance, you may want to consider working with a financial advisor. Financial advisors can help you create a customized financial plan and provide guidance on topics such as budgeting, saving, debt management, and investing.

- **Books:** There are many books available on personal finance that can provide valuable insights and strategies. Some popular options include "The Total Money Makeover" by Dave Ramsey and "Your Money or Your Life" by Vicki Robin.

By taking advantage of these resources, you can continue to learn and grow in your financial journey.

In this book, we have covered a range of topics related to good financial management, including budgeting, saving, debt management, and investing. By implementing these strategies and making informed decisions about your money, you can take control of your financial life and work towards a secure financial future.

Remember, good financial management is a journey, not a destination. It's important to be patient and consistent in your approach and to continuously review and adjust your financial plan as your circumstances change.

This is hoping that the information and strategies presented in this book have been helpful in getting you started on your financial journey. With the right mindset and a solid plan in place, you can solve your money problems now and get your money right!

www.ingramcontent.com/pod-product-compliance
Lightning Source LLC
Chambersburg PA
CBHW050322220526
45465CB00005B/2095